WOE TO THE LAND SHADOWING

POEMS

RED SHUTTLEWORTH

BLUE HORSE PRESS REDONDO BEACH, CALIFORNIA 2015

WOE TO THE LAND SHADOWING

RED SHUTTLEWORTH

Blue Horse Press
P.O. Box 7000 - 760
Redondo Beach,
California   90277

Cover art: Ciara Shuttleworth

Editors: Jeffrey and Tobi Alfier
Blue Horse Press logo: Amy Lynn Hayes

ISBN 978-0692560457

Acknowledgments:

The poems in this collection were first presented, some in slightly different versions, on my blog: poetredshuttleworth.blogspot.com.

Many of the poems were included in the following (exceptionally limited edition) Bunchgrass Press chapbooks:

Hearken

What Can We Make of This?

Ghost Window

An Extra Blue Mile

Pinto Ridge

Final Light of Day

Campsites of Ghosts

Special thanks to Ciara Shuttleworth for a close reading, counsel, and some editing.

For

Maura, Ciara, Luke, and Jessi

Contents

too late to brighten the sky

Samuel Beckett, *Eneug II*

Hearken

At the hard-brown sunflower stalk edge
of a sage steppe town, withered poplars,
abandoned single-wide trailers, September
finishes cool and rainy, a begged-for kiss:
blackbirds flutter-mad in a field of cut alfalfa.

Blueberry Muffin Sky… Another Swallow of Cherry Coke

You're counting oncoming cars and trucks:
thirty-three between Soap Lake and Ephrata.
How easy to swerve across a center line
while mulling over how coyotes
quickly acquire a taste for sick llama.
The only yellow canine eyes ahead
are between royal-blue clouds.

The state is privatizing the sale of booze.
Coming soon to Safeway: long stemmed
white roses between bottles of Wild Turkey.
That's what you suggest to the clerk
who wonders why, at age seventy,
you give a crap if the Hershey bars are fresh.

At Ace Hardware a breasty young blonde
helps you find a package of D-rings,
says she can't go home tonight, *My mom's
there with her new boyfriend who works
sometimes at the auto parts store.*

It's human to seek borders…
to treat memories as if they are plastic
toys to be thrown off walls.
You like the idea of *making* memories,
so you offer what you hope can pass
as a dangerous famished-coyote smile
to the hardware girls… something close
to a three-chord country-guitar song.

The hound behind you in the back seat,
enormous head out the car window,
will never attend a funeral, a wedding,
or walk into Safeway and gaze,
pissed-off, at the syrup-romance
paperbacks written by hacks…
while considering the 14% jump
in the price of brown rice in two months.

Counting oncoming cars and trucks
in the reverse direction, you drive slower
so that the numbers increase.

The Situation Only Appears Familiar

Our scabland has fallen from the moon…
a meal some *Revelations* monster refused to eat.

Sitting at a window of a tumbledown
beef country hotel, you want something to happen.

Hitched to stumbling ways, the dying goes on…
with every call out of the alfalfa-green phone.

Carried forward:
an attachment for self-reprisals.

Gold sun, honey skin, kisses… love-groans.
You're only good, she giggled, *for one thing*.

You ran off too many sweet girls,
using Edvard Munch's notion

about paintings left in blizzards,
It does them good to fend for themselves.

Vegas: hundreds of tequila bottles back.
The Great Plains? Countless whiskey ditches ago.

Trinket Glare

A stranger weighs local soil in stiff hands.
A silver ring glows from tall brown weeds.
The emporium of defects never closes.

Eyelids feel the fast-rising white sun.
Who will start the breakfast fire?
A dust devil whips sunflowers off
the front of a mud-splattered house.

A girl with glazed blue skin undresses,
listens to handwritten letters on the floor:
songs of Sunday love... graveyard Sundays.

A *Help Wanted* sign drops from a cloud.
Half a desk chair falls from another cloud.
Blight-tomatoes, gray summer squash,
a black tea cup: it is raining inside of time.

Postscript

Century-old unmarked graves in a dry coulee.
A man grinds one rock upon another for driveway pebbles.

At a cold window, a doctor's narrow face appears pained
as he scrubs marble-white hands over a clogged, bloody sink.

From outhouses to four-hundred dollar plumbing bills
in just fifty years! A crazy shrink waits online with salty answers.

A horsewoman comes down the grave road on an Arabian mare.
The woman's sharp tongue rises up to her drippy nose.

The silence of rock-shattered ancient Indian skulls.
The sun makes a late appearance, trembles... plunges.

Revelations Sunday

Virus-colored geese cross a storm sky.
You gather coils of rusty barb wire
left by the last man who failed on this
rock-'n-rattler sagebrush ground.
Lightning cracks ten miles southwest.

~

You drive restless-slow to the creek and back home…
six miles of scab rock. You don't step out of the rig
at a shotgun-executed refrigerator… a dog hidden,
skeleton for sure by now, beneath a Christmas
tree from last year. You drive with eyes closed
where you know there's straight gravel road.
You drive as if in a faded color photograph
saved from the 1950's, windows down,
Stetson straw pulled low to shadow your eyes.

As Months Merge

Slaughterhouse nap-dreams... brass bullets
straight to swine-squeal foreheads.
You have been reading newspapers,
barrel-bomb stories set in Syria or Iraq,
sidebar crucifixions, beheadings,
runaway London teens crossing
the porous border from Turkey to....
Now your east window is cracked open
to a starry night... some thick-haired
dwarf planet entering human consciousness.
So many natural wonders... neglect or appreciate.
You awaken sweaty, crusty-eyed, not yourself...
neither protagonist or antagonist, nor deciding agent.

What Can We Make of This?

Plastic pouch of dried, sugary blueberries
to help keep off Copenhagen-with-bourbon,
the Wolfhound happily back seat grinning
from an open window, you slow drive...
watch neighbors disc thawing fields.

No effect in wrestling with CNN news:
ISIS tosses gays off Syrian roofs,
New York/London Fashion Week
and leather accessories, a Delta jet
skids off a snowy New York runway.
The jasmine scent of a certain Delta
stewardess comes sweet-memory back...
grace and poignancy of a motel bar drink.

Early March on a lonesome sage steppe...
mourning doves in non-native evergreens,
fifty degree afternoons for baseball,
contrails of Navy fighters thundering
from Whidbey to Mountain Home.

Half a Milk Bone at every stop,
a mile walk every hour and a half.
A young Wolfhound and an old man
ride-out a swayback sunny afternoon.

Shrub Desert… Individuality

Airplane crash ghosts
crow-scream into so many memories
until those who remember are also ghosts.

Today a blue-lavender sky.

This evening a cheap predator
whistle to play a rabbit-in-agony
song for local coyotes.

A Door is Going to Open

Morning of grass wedding rings....

Bile-yellow clouds drift east.

A hemp ladder rises to a loft
in a small desert town hotel.

Your ghosts ballet-twirl,
throw silvery dust,

a pale bird,
no larger than the heel of a child's hand,
curves toward April poplars.

Your fate is drawn fast to a snubbin' post.

Lack of Grasp: Furnished Rooms… Weekly Rates

Gaudy stanchions at the nearest strip mall.
Shallow-neck pink cotton dresses.

A woman at a ghost window
sets Doc Holliday's memoirs on an oak desk.

Red-'n-blue Christmas tree
lights in a Columbia Basin cantina.

Moose horns over a cabin door.
Teardrops on a buffalo hide travel bag.

She remarks, *Velour-soft places for the rankled.*
Too-late radio love songs… back porch moonlight.

Platter of Almost-Sunrise

Heaven of half-remembered cow towns…
you're swinging off lard-greased chandeliers.

Some angel took a fence stretcher to your skull,

Global warming is so evident you can rope it.

Old West nostalgia narrows
to downhill accountants, fake-desperado frock coats,
writing flat-word pulp novels.

Or Roy Rogers,
in black Hades boots,
stomps Dale.

Semis bleed the freeway to Spokane.
Three roadside dead at three in the morning.

Ronny Elliott on satellite radio,
Tell the Killer the King is Dead.

The present disappears…
arc of stone's throw.

On Track

I walk… sometimes lope
a .3-mile track in my sagebrushy north pasture.

Oh, the rapture of coyote laughter.
Solemn crows offer weak perspective
to sweep sunlight.

Though he does not know it, Wang Wei
walks beside me, huffing and puffing poems.

My body contains Mongolian and Gaelic rain.

At seventy a man names horses he will not
ride to the end of this powdered-bone century.

Sometimes I jog a few steps to feel the wreckage
we are born towards… to steal lies from the dead.

Stay or Go

Along with a sand-wind to grit dishes,
a squabble of hawks in a sad claimants
titanium-blue sky.

Not-right-now marionberry
cafe pie... dead flies
in the dust of a display case.

The looted aquifers....
No one knows anymore...
not for sure.

Ambulance on Highway #17

You tell your erstwhile friend
it's like being inside the last air bubble
in a dry cleaner's bag… the judgmental
part left undone. The siren draws
attention to the quirky-slow roll
of a meat wagon emergency.

You consider all the poetry
classes left in pine drawers…
handwritten syllabuses…
scraps of legal pads…
monastery lampshade-yellow.

Sunlight-Scatter... Saturday

This overarching happiness
is a fresh-painted red truck on gravel...
an empty cattle trailer rattling behind it.
All that rust shaken off... windblown.

Tomorrow I shall get up at four a.m.,
drive to Walla Walla, listen to Russell
sing *Blue Wing* over and over again.
Tomorrow: snapshots of drought country,
lines in a red-as-lifeblood notebook.

It will be Sunday tomorrow...
like day-old roadside shell casings.
This happiness will be a chalky memory.

Planted Ground

Grotesque turn of tractor
and a leg is gone:
someone else's fact.
Wood clouds… a radio song
featuring high platform heels,
love gone to muscatel-sobs.
For you it's morning…
dryland wheat fields
at every blacktop
curve-'n-swerve…
graveyard rows.

The Future Seemed Chandelier-Spectacular

Morning comes at you
like a sloganeering nun
in a Clint Eastwood movie…
desert radio jangle,
some *furniture festival* in town.
You carry all the ephemera
of seventy years…
smeared postcard postscripts.

Pockmarked moon through squinty eyes….
Peaches-the-Wolfhound wants to know:
when does she get the lapis-blue
birthday present leather collar?

On a grand scale of gnarled apple tree
to gloss-marble of gunfighter boot hill,
the flake-decay centerpiece would be
a Bat Masterson toupee up for auction.

Before the Hand of

Spilled beer and Jesus-platitudes,
road-twisted cheap-brass rodeo trophy buckle....
And the pickup rattles...
fencing tools and crushed beer cans.

Red wildfire-sun,
three roadside crosses in one downhill mile,
illegal burn barrel with a smokin' garden hose....

It's a drought-year nothin'.
Just sit sullen on a padded oak rockin' chair...
fire a nickel-plated seven-inch Colt revolver,
all the .45 rounds you can afford, into a neighbor's
center pivot section of gene-combo corn.

Bramble-Night

It is said by the more frank
craftsmen of a certain passion,
Death masks are self-creations.

Transcontinental phone calls, midnight pleading,
drives to and from Las Vegas… diamond-shaped
sugar-crystal tears of lovers drunk on boutique bottles,
cheapest tequila… samplers for the manic.

You're swimming a murky green pool—
moonless night—at an abandoned limestone quarry.

Or night falls from Wyoming iron clouds,
comes down as horseshoes…
and you lean back in a greasy plastic booth
in Little America… wait for scrambled eggs..
and you feel safe from yourself… for a while.

The Core of Our Moon is Iron

Miles traveled are points in a game of mistakes.
The sun rises bronzy… soon turns brimstone-yellow.

The little faces the sky makes jiggle and jump…
and it's a joke for some dry-humor god.

And within recall:
The rumble of fractured bottom ground,
rock climbing rock to new elevation.

Lily skin, lavender shawl, tight greenish jeans,
Go… we should go <u>somewhere</u>. She also said,

Nobody <u>really</u> feeds the heart-sprawled…
certainly not little banjo players. On the corners.

You sit, flask of bourbon-water:
the sun thrill-rises sulfuric
through basalt dust and grass-fire, sagebrush smoke.

Collapse of Stacked-up Details

You dream rattlers…
drinking caffeine-rich soda pop
from your dog's stainless steel supper bowl.

Dry grass… wildfire weeks…
you quick-buy a nebulizer.

The Wolfhound wants to sit
for a strip of old-style photo booth portraits…
wants you to plunk the last car-change
quarters into some chewing-gummed slot.

A best friend drops into a diabetic blackout
while driving home with Chinese take-out,
crashes into a parked dildo-Lexus… totals it.
Not much later comes the small stroke…
loss of vision in the left eye…
the one that best saw a ninety-plus
baseball coming 60-feet from the bump.

Blue haze… mourning doves
forever in nonlinear time and space…
wildfire smoke and bird-screech.

Age seventy's residue….
You're just another dust devil.

Sunday Desert Approach

Forget economy-of-time:
last night's wishful
dream-swatches…
lapis lazuli velvet.

You wish to imagine
purple heather.
Sagebrush drops
pale shade
too morning-cool
for rattlers.

Oh… the showmanship of hawks.

Dry Coulee: 1

Likewise… wildfire smoke
text messages ancient volcanic rock.
Such is sincerity, the living close
to each other. Art Deco fridges,
stained glass wall hangings,
camp-outs… the inkjet life…
all of it up in black-'n-white.

Dry Coulee: 2

Clutching-foolish to rusty barb wire coils,
you nightmare-run a flaming apple orchard…
scent of grassy burned pie crust.

Dream alone… dream alone… dream alone:
flaming Bible pages in a scorch-wind.

One oily sagebrush at a time torches-up.

You nightmare-run along train tracks…
train gone east a century ago…
moon-white pony and bison skulls.

Dry Coulee: 3

Don't sun-glance, not through smoke,
even with blue-tint Oakley lenses.
A dim past—gray ceramic pioneer figurines—
rides a smoke-snake against rock.
You step from the car with the Wolfhound
for a bite of charred air. The coulees
have acquired a rough black collar.
A deer gasps across a gravel road…
lurches into a drought-fringe of bunch grass,
stumbles on fire-charred scree, looks back.

Pinto Ridge

Fire-displaced coyotes, kangaroo rats,
deer… all scowl-southward in haze-desert.
You hike, today's mystery guest
for those who keep an eye out:
rattler… deranged woodpecker.

Smoke-rouge at sundown…
then the sky going dark…
a blank-ash TV screen.

No more than a speck of dust
to a distant, throw-away old horse,
you hike, listen for blind cars
on a lonesome two-lane,
take slugs of water
from a cheap canteen,
swallow against loss.

Clapboard Day

If the wildfire smoke/haze would blow
elsewhere you could do voice-overs.
Keep in mind the Big Bang… fire and smoke
we cannot telescope-witness.

Typically, the readership is a hidden thread.

You are dog-reminded:
every eloquent hillbilly song, rustic fairy tale,
serves to confirm… you never could
stay within machine-ruled lines…
never were meant to earn good grades.

First Cold Front of Summer

Darkening alfalfa fields past second cutting,
pastures, cattle juggling last light on short horns.
Twenty-two miles south, the freeway is closed.
First cold front of summer is whipping through.

Evening, dirty-heavy gusts at 40,
you're on a three-mile daydream,
walking ghost Wolfhounds on a canal road.
Later: ice cubes and glacier water in crystal.

Existence divides into small particles.
Radio reportage: blowing dust and smoke....
The bloody freeway-injured at Silica Road
are kept moaning in wrecked pick-ups and cars.

The Least Bit

Trance-like driving after three hours
on a car lot... pencil notes on showroom gloss.
You are brain-numb... fit to be padlocked.

At kitchen counter, you butter soda crackers,
one for the Wolfhound, one for you...
one for the Wolfhound, two for you....

So many of us are misrepresentations.
Many of us are capitulations or refusals.

Ambiguous clouds build in the west,
white-splatter atop old-town steel.
Below all of it...more wildfire smoke/haze.

You're weary of navigation, of dashboard maps
jabbing your eyes with sorry location.

Final Light of Day

Twist of rusty barb wire, failed grids,
goat-cleared brushy pasture… sagebrush….
You listen for a passenger jet…
Seattle to Boston? Pilots with available
oxygen masks in the shadows
of old lovers' apartments….

You listen for jet rumble to drop
36,000 feet to where you're taking snapshots
of over-grazed, August sage steppe.
Night is quirky-falling, ash-gray
from the wildfire surrounding Chelan.

Stepping against a weather-broken fence
some other unshaven old man put up…
to have something to watch while dying,
you scan for where horizon might be,
where a sun might be ill-burning inward.

Wildfire Smoke/Haze... Sky Smudges

Commonality: cell phones on-silent
from burned-out towns on the Columbia River.

You wake to semi-darkness before sundown...
a listing-sideways evening without sun or cloud.

Hypnagogic voices jerk in unlike song... in scream.

You fly awake before dawn...
taste of charred power pole from up north.

Outside with a huffing Wolfhound
in sky-smothered ashy darkness...
you twist open every farmyard hydrant.

A mourning dove, bleached bone, shrieks past.

Crescent of Blood Where We Expected the Moon

Chronology seems old fashioned…
a sky of creamy ash. Quivering sun.
Vocabulary hits a washboard road.

Vocabulary in grays…
a gone-circus… a leathery underside
of our oversize 1950's clown shoes.

What is it that hovers among particulates
of inferno-forest? Memories of lilac
lingerie… cool touch of a fog-blue tin cup?

Canal Road Southeast of Adrian,
Washington... Four Miles at Sunset

Less smoke/haze: the muscular sun,
red-lacquered and thumping crazy for weeks,
releases us from daylight... falls, falls, falls....

Head down, you listen to eerie magpie cries
filtered through pine-ash particulates:
West Nile Virus, Feathers of West Nile Virus....

Luminous black-glow: August is dying,
painted pony-cough... coyote croak.
Nightmare-splatter gravel.

Smoke Shadows at Eye Level

Origins in some god's dance hall fire…
birth from ancient cosmic outward wind….

You are driving smoke-blind,
coughing, looking for head-on chrome.

You are wearing a Halloween skeleton costume…
topped with a black wide-brim Resistol hat.

Or… you are six deer in crimson brake lights.
The ash-carpeting of heaven is badger-gnawed.

Campsites of Ghosts

You drag yourself and your sidekick Wolfhound,
grainy wildfire-particulates air, for another
sagebrush walk. North, in front of flames,
deer, badger, back-scorched coyote…
the last wild pony… run for their lives.

Pale orange sun at bacon-cheese noon.
The Wolfhound hard-sneezes black smoke grit.
It's on your plate. Then you're on a crumbled
blacktop road through dead bunch grass,
the hound circling haunted stone circles.

You tell your friend, *Mouth's so dry…*
could use a bulge of Red Man chewin' tobacco.
The lead-white/gray sky turns ash-yellow.
The weight of each minute is a saddlebag
of ripped cotton shirts wrapping bone.

Sky-Ashes Poem…
With Irish Wolfhound… Again

Scribbly weeds,
gone-youth under funerary clouds.

The Wolfhound huffs, *Promises…promises.*...

We walk… cough-trot in death-haze…
ash of pine… ash of black bear with cubs….

Feeling Superimposed

Darkening alfalfa fields…
quilt for the hospice-placed.

Foreboding-gold sun…
band of red… charcoal sky.

You want toasted black bread
after this four-mile hike…
lather of strawberry preserves.

Daydream: a Rawlings infielder mitt,
candy-hop grounders to catch and toss.

Memory: a Santee coyote mask
in a Cedar City, Utah, curio shop.

Daydream: a laughing
treadmill-addicted stage actress…
chocolate cake, bourbon, a motel room.

Night sky, we are the offspring of stars?

Woe to the Land Shadowing

Less evening wildfire smoke from the north...
and you step into the path of a black car,
no headlights, ten minutes past sundown.

You're listening to the laughter
of twenty-five years ago:
loopy-drunk rodeo girls in striped shirts
unsnapped to black-ribbon turquoise bras.

You're following a center pivot's
far nozzle over late August alfalfa...
shower of glacier-cold ancient water.

You're not yourself... a voice inside
a dust-clogged old fashioned telephone
on a filling station wall... you're not yourself.

A no-headlights black car blares
a horn... brushes past on blacktop.
You're alive... post-rumble upright,
whiff of gasoline... baled alfalfa.

Always Trying to Make Country Singer Parallels

Brief reunions… old lovers at sunrise:
1980's radio static, medicinal-purpose whiskey,
echo-drip of a missile silo pipe thirty miles east.

If showers from the Pacific weaken…
in case… in case Chelan fully burns,
you work toward a palette of smoke colors:
raccoon-blood smoke… lemon-sky haze.

Night grazing horses, baled alfalfa
a mile west in pie crust light…
nothing explains pebbles in running shoes
or how far you keep at stutter-jog before….

Or the lovers are honorary mayors
in rubble-thick villages, age-withered…
with gold cardboard keys to nothing.

Thin Strips of Bed Sheet Tied to Barb Wire

Out back of a boarded trailer,
scattered deer bones from poach years,
bright tricycle bars
poking up from drought grass,
a no-engine, no-tires Econoline Van….

There are worse places to drink.
A wife blows bathtub bubbles,
manic hums, starts scissoring more
than colored paper cut-out dolls.
But you follow her to Gilroy.

Paved road, nearly eight acres,
good well, stove not used
in the last dozen years.
Jaundice yellow-gray sky.
Call realtor before looking.

Ephemeral Sky… Evening

Miles north of the last patchy lawn
of a shrub steppe town, a hapless
flock of chalk-yellow birds….

Gentle early September wind
and you suffer a stainless steel
daydream as you bridge-rattle
across an irrigation canal.

Wood power poles stride
toward the fiery north…
pop of arthritic spines.

In the southbound lane,
store-fresh, bakery-wrapped,
hotdog buns on blacktop…
not quite road kill… not yet.

Hundreds of Miles Between

Pamphlet-speak: grassland-ruined-to-sagebrush.
You're driving… loose, a silhouette of youth.
A singer on CD boasts bar fight… lost love.

~

Deep blue sky over cast iron clouds.
Ages of anxiety… ages of aggression: no rain.
Another coyote September, non-Alpha pups
sent loping off, no-pack nomads… hungry.

~

Wind-blown splinter off an old corral board,
you're safe from bank vault gloss… employment.
You're on-the-scout for a whiskey-'n-rainwater.

~

Black-'n-starry cosmos, click-'n-ping satellites…
memory of cow town gospel-pink topless angels.
Twenty-four years past broke-crystal-ball Vegas…
you night drive… shard-glass steering wheel.

Gravel over Rock

Deadbone humor… broke-mirror ghosts…
black sunshine on the moon,
concussions… hemorrhages ahead…
if cheap-luck doesn't change.

Almost night… goddess-headed
sagebrush comes alive with rising coyotes.

You are kicked over sober
these months… manic note taker,
mailer of crumpled-corner postcards.

Shot glass of bourbon skipped,
you thin-slice a banana… top it
with midnight's whipped cream.
Seventy, you claim you're *youngish*?

Mirror-Distorted Pastoral Dream

Phone rings… dice shake in a plastic cup:
you learn there's yellow-gold sky over Vegas.
Crushed cigarette packs, forced smiles,
grimy used-before wedding rice:
the lonesome of memory-left-behind.

You listen, drawn-in: someone else's stroke,
someone else's dialysis, a friend too rickety
to shuffle across a living room without falling.

Now you grip a fistful of volcanic ash
from three-inches below surface soil.
Now your blood is sober… no conclusion.

Phone is silent. Your knee-high,
mule-eared Tony Lama boots scuff hardwood.
The window is open to drought-tough sagebrush,
to coyote scream, to blacktop a mile or two
closer to some ditch wreck… to Nevada.

Tall Corn, Blue Roses, Rusted Kids' Swing

Orange harvest-month candle
in a store window… a screw-up
former bank clerk selling bike chains,
used motel soap bars, old screen doors:
you drive through town, at the limit.

A box of black & white negatives,
loose postcards from Copenhagen,
North Platte, an Elko whorehouse,
dusty-drops from a closet shelf.

Strangers with slices of blood-cake….
Against sleep, you begin to write
a snakebite, no anti-venom available
one-act play: it's someone's birthday.
A shortage of prom queen pedestals….

You daydream yourself an airport
beside a leafy river… locust thorn trees.
You stroll a farm sale, old implements,
bulge-eyed children hacking thistle….

Rattlesnake Sunfall

Mysterious… savage…
jiggle-buttons…

wide-jaw…
glisten of setting
sun… fangs…

float-'n-folkloric…
snap.

Midnight Gape

I

Legacy… leathery chestnut eyes
amid flickering candles….

Shaggy-feathered owl.

A generality of heydays
bleeds to a monochromatic bloodpool.

II

It's so easy to quote the sixties
from the pallor of *Vogue* girls…

(Idealized love poems
are for stucco hearts.)

throwback rock babes
explicit with whipped cream eggs.

Change of Weather Night

Shimmering emulation of life...
a couple million light years away.

Here it's erosive cell phones...
absence of bison-dream recall.

You coyote-stare at a slice
of pulse-dead purple star.

You hanker for rabbit
stroganoff from an iron skillet.

The sky swirls black...
flowing ghost robes.

Boreal Bone

Cold-drip night: a crazy deer bursts
from dark-ice with a lucky charms necklace.

You never did figure out how to turn on
the hydrant of change… time just a nudge off.

Bargain Sundays, crippled feedlot cattle
better off with a bullet, angel kisses in the rain.

Then there's the town: goof music from boombox
cars with homemade spoiler screwed to trunks.

You blow the plastic predator whistle: rabbit
scream, rain, vomit, rain, dream sermons…

and years pass and you can't get over anything.
You paint and bubble wrap it, send it to strangers.

About the Author

Red Shuttleworth is a three-time recipient of the Spur Award (from Western Writers of America) for Poetry: *Johnny Ringo* (2013), *Roadside Attractions* (2011) and *Western Settings* (2001). Shuttleworth was named "Best Living Western Poet" in 2007 by *True West* magazine. His poetry and short plays have appeared in numerous journals, including *Alaska Quarterly Review*, *Concho River Review*, *Los Angeles Review*, *Ontario Review*, *Prairie Schooner*, *South Dakota Review,* and *Weber: The Contemporary West*. Shuttleworth's plays on the West have been presented widely, including at The State University of New York at Fredonia, Sundance Playwrights Lab, The Sun Valley Festival of New Western Drama, and the Tony Award-winning Utah Shakespearean Festival.

www.ingramcontent.com/pod-product-compliance
Lightning Source LLC
Chambersburg PA
CBHW072053040426
42447CB00012BB/3102